Food Like Mine

My name is

. . . .

My favourite food is

. . . .

Alonso, aged 9,
Mexico

Hafsa, aged 7,
South Africa

DK

DK | Penguin Random House

Senior Editor Carrie Love

Editor Sophia Danielsson-Waters

Senior Designers Lisa Robb, Elaine Hewson

Designers Rachael Hare, Pauline Marie Korp

Food Photographer Dave King

Home Economist and Recipe Writer Denise Smart

Jacket Designer Lisa Robb

Jacket Co-ordinator Francesca Young

Pre-production Producer Nadine King

Producer Isabell Schart

Creative Technical Support Sonia Charbonnier

Managing Editor Penny Smith

Managing Art Editors Mabel Chan, Gemma Glover

Publisher Mary Ling

Creative Director Jane Bull

Consultants Michael Blake (Maize),
Annie Gray (Other staples), Stephen Harris (Wheat),
Renee Marton (Rice), and Andrew Smith (Potatoes)

First published in Great Britain in 2017 by
Dorling Kindersley Limited
80 Strand, London WC2R 0RL

10 9 8 7 6 5 4 3 2 1

001-285428-July/2017

A CIP catalogue record for this book is available
from the British Library.

ISBN: 978-0-2412-3097-8

Printed and bound in China

Discover more at www.dk.com

⚠ Please note

All the recipes in this book are to be made under adult
supervision. When you see the warning triangle, take
extra care as hot cookers, electrical appliances, and
sharp implements are used in making a recipe.
Ask an adult to help you.

Kitchen rules

- When you're in the kitchen, you should ask an adult
to move things in and out of the oven and to heat
things on the hob.
- Ask an adult to help if you need to use a sharp knife
or an electrical appliance.
- Wash your hands before and after you work with
food. Always wash your hands after handling raw
eggs and raw meat.
- Do not lick your fingers when you are working
with food.
- Check the use-by date on all ingredients.
- Follow the instructions on packaging on how
to store food.

Getting started

1. Read the recipe instructions all the way through
before you begin.
2. Gather together everything you need.
3. Have a cloth handy to mop up spillages.
4. Put on an apron, tie back your hair, and wash
your hands.

Key to symbols

 How many people a dish **serves**, or how
many portions it **makes**.

 The time it takes to **prepare** a dish, including
chilling and marinating.

 The time it takes to **cook** a dish.

CONTENTS

Jamie, aged 8, New Zealand

Erel, aged 7, Israel

The world of FOOD

Food is about more than just eating. It shows who we are, where we come from, and what we like. Eating habits are shaped by our culture and beliefs. Even what we eat for breakfast may seem strange to someone on the other side of the world. But one thing's certain – we're all united by food!

> More than one **TRILLION** chicken eggs are laid every year.

Ivan, aged 7, Malaysia

Joaquin, aged 11, USA

Uncooked white **RICE** can last for up to **10** years.

There are **1.5 BILLION** cows in the world.

Clara, aged 9, Germany

MAIZE SYRUP can be found in **TOMATO SAUCE, SOFT DRINKS,** and **YOGURT.**

POTATOES were the first food grown in **SPACE.**

The **spiciness** of chilli peppers is measured on a scale called **SCOVILLES.**

Trini, aged 10, Argentina

Joshua, aged 8, Botswana

Types of FOOD

There are five main types of food. They help your body with different things and all have a job to do. Food gives you the energy to play, run, think and grow. The biggest source of this energy comes from carbohydrates.

Portion advice varies, but a variety of different foods is healthy.

Jollof rice

Carbohydrates

Carbohydrates are starchy foods that usually come from grains (rice, wheat, maize, rye, barley, and oats). There are other sources too, including vegetables and some fruits.

Bread

Select wholegrain varieties as they are healthier.

Carbohydrates help your muscles and organs to work well.

Brown rice

Couscous

Noodles

Oats

Pasta dish

Rye

Maize

Breakfast cereal

Yam

Sweet potato

Potato

Fruit and vegetables

This food group provides you with fibre, vitamins, and minerals. Fruit and vegetables help your body to heal itself, to prevent infections, and keep your skin healthy.

Apple

Cabbage

Pumpkin

Mandarin orange

Tomato

Runner beans

Protein

Protein is found in meat, but also in non-animal sources. Protein-rich foods help your body to repair and to grow.

Foods high in protein often contain vitamins and minerals too.

Chicken

Egg

Lentils

Lamb is a great source of B vitamins.

Fish

Lamb

Peas

Beans

Soybeans

Nuts

Milk and dairy

This food group is high in calcium, which helps your nerves and muscles work well and strengthens your teeth and bones.

Fats help to maintain body heat and transport vitamins around your body.

Fats

It's best to choose foods containing healthy fats, such as the ones shown below.

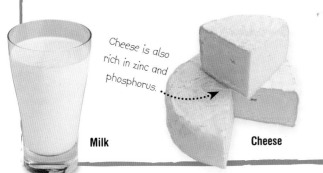

Cheese is also rich in zinc and phosphorus.

Olives

Oily fish

Avocado

Milk

Cheese

Yogurt

What are STAPLE foods?

Staple foods are the filling foods people eat regularly around the world – sometimes as part of every meal. They give us a large amount of calories, and are generally easy to grow and store. Even better, they're usually cheap to buy, accessible all year round, and won't spoil quickly. With all these positives, it's no wonder we eat them so much!

The **four** main staples are all edible plants. There are about **200,000** edible plants in the world, but only **0.1%** are regularly eaten by people.

1

Rice is eaten regularly by more than half the people in the world.

RICE

2

Wheat is used to make bread, which is eaten almost everywhere.

WHEAT

3

Maize is especially important in the Americas.

MAIZE

POTATOES

Potatoes are eaten by more than a billion people worldwide.

4

Other staples are **legumes**, certain **fruits, meat, fish, dairy**, and some **root vegetables**.

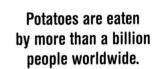

RICE

This tiny grain is eaten in every country in the world. It is an integral part of our diet and provides us with lots of energy. In many countries, rice is eaten at every mealtime and as a snack. It's a key part of our past and an even more important part of our future.

The continent that grows the **MOST** rice is **ASIA.**

Rice is eaten **TWICE** a day by **two thirds** of the world's population.

When rice is cooked it swells to **3 times** its original **WEIGHT.**

There are more than **100,000** varieties of **rice** grown in the world.

Rice was used to strengthen the Great **WALL** of China.

Rice is used in lots of **COSMETICS.**

FIELDS OF RICE

Rice needs a lot of water to grow. Farmers often flood the land they want to grow rice on, or use land that is already flooded to ensure a good crop. These flooded areas are called "paddy fields".

Ducks and fish often live in paddy fields. They eat pests and weeds that would otherwise harm the rice plants.

RICE is important for the FUTURE as it can withstand a slight rise in global temperature, whereas WHEAT and MAIZE will struggle more.

Growing RICE

Rice is primarily grown in paddy fields and terraces around the world. It usually takes 3-4 months to grow, from planting the seedlings to harvesting the grains. Rice is milled before it is cooked and eaten.

Growing rice

The soil in a field or terrace is **ploughed** and **tilled** (dug up and mixed together), then levelled back out. Then rice seedlings are planted by hand or machine. Once the rice is fully grown, it's gathered by hand or by a combine harvester.

Seedling

Harvesting by hand

Nearly 95% of all RICE is EATEN in the country where it is grown.

Rice plant

Harvesting by machine

The part of rice that we eat is called the grain (also called the seed)

Bran

Hull

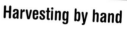

From paddy to plate

Before rice can be eaten, it must be dried out and go through a milling process. The grain is separated from the hull (hard outer casing) as well as the bran layer. However, if brown rice is desired, the bran layer is left on the grain. Otherwise, you get white rice.

Types of rice

There are more than 40,000 varieties of rice, but they all fall into two main categories – Asian rice and African rice. All rice is described by the length of its grain once it's been cooked (short, medium, or long).

Rice comes in lots of colours: white, brown, purple, red, and black.

Uses for rice

Rice is often ground into flour and used to make a variety of foods such as noodles, paper rolls, and cakes. Rice can also be puffed and made into cereal and crackers.

Rice flour

Fresh rice noodles

DELICIOUS DOSAS

These folded pancakes are made from rice flour and lentils. They are eaten as a snack or as a meal.

Dosa

Dried rice noodles

Another common way of describing rice is by whether it's "sticky" or "less-sticky" once it's cooked.

Rice is heated in a circular mould and puffs up to fill the space. ....

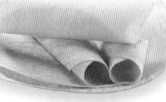

Rice paper rolls

Puffed rice cereal

These rice cakes are eaten at Chinese New Year. ....

Rice cracker

Sweet rice cakes

Short-grain

Also called "round grain rice", short-grain rice is up to 5mm (⅕in) long. This type always sticks together when it's cooked.

Short-grain rice is used to make sushi, sweet rice dishes, porridge, and dumplings.

Camargue red rice

Arborio rice

American short-grain rice

Like Asian rice, African rice has short-, medium-, and long-grain varieties.

Medium-grain

Medium-grain rice is 5.2mm-6mm (⅕-¼in). The grains are tender and moist and usually cling together when cooked.

Medium-grain rice may be used for paellas and creamy rice desserts.

This type contains lots of iron.

Brown standard rice

Spanish bomba rice

Chinese black rice

Long-grain

Any rice that is 6mm (¼in) or longer is called long-grain. This rice can be white or brown and is light and fluffy when cooked.

Jasmine rice

Long-grain rice is ideal for making side dishes, soups, pilafs, salads, and stuffings.

Basmati rice has a nut-like flavour.

Basmati rice

Red cargo

American long-grain rice

Whether it's in a main meal or used in sweet treats or snacks, you can always rely on rice. There are rice dishes for every time of day, from breakfast, to lunch and dinner.

Daifuku, Japan

This Japanese sweet treat is made from mochi – a sticky rice cake that is pounded into a paste. It has a sweet bean filling, called anko.

RICE around

Kedgeree, UK

This spiced rice and lentil dish is often eaten for breakfast, and usually contains smoked fish, such as haddock.

Khalifa, aged 6, Bahrain

Qoozi, Bahrain

Qoozi is popular in Bahrain and the countries nearby. It's a dish of lamb, nuts, currants, and vegetables, all served on a bed of rice.

Songpyeon, South Korea

These rice cakes are stuffed with a sweet or savoury filling. They are commonly eaten at a Korean harvest festival celebration.

Yeh-Lin, aged 9, South Korea

Arancini, Italy

Crunchy outside and soft inside, arancini are breaded rice balls that are deep fried. They are usually eaten as an appetiser or snack.

the world

Cooked white rice

Naiyarat (Knight), aged 8, Thailand

Pad thai, Thailand

A popular street food in Thailand, pad thai is a mixture of rice noodles, firm tofu, vegetables, and often seafood.

Biryani, India

Basmati rice is the main ingredient of this savoury meal. Biryani can contain meat, fish, or vegetables, and is spiced differently from region to region.

Lucas, aged 6, Spain

Paella, Spain

This dish mixes rice with seafood, vegetables, or chicken and sausages. It's cooked in a large, shallow pan and comes from Valencia in Spain.

Congee, China

This is a creamy rice porridge dish. It's a comfort food and is popular all over the world – especially in Asia.

Vegetable sushi rolls

These rice rolls are filled with vegetables and wrapped in seaweed. They are served with pickled ginger, wasabi paste, and soy sauce.

YOU WILL NEED:

- *bamboo mat*
- *250g (9oz) sushi rice*
- *325ml (11 fl oz) jug of water*
- *2 tbsp white wine vinegar*
- *1 tbsp caster sugar*
- *½ tsp table salt*
- *¼ cucumber*
- *½ small carrot*
- *½ small red pepper*
- *½ small yellow pepper*
- *4 nori (seaweed) sheets*

TO SERVE:

- *pickled ginger*
- *soy sauce*
- *wasabi paste (optional)*

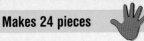
1

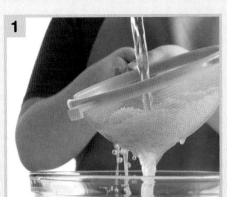

Rinse the rice with cold water, until the water runs clear. Put the rice in a pan. Add water from the jug.

2

Bring the rice to the boil. Reduce the heat and cover. Simmer for 10 minutes. Remove from the heat and leave to steam.

3

Meanwhile, warm the vinegar, sugar, and salt in a small pan until they dissolve.

4

Spread the rice onto a metal tray. Pour the vinegar mixture evenly over the rice and gently mix. Leave to cool.

5

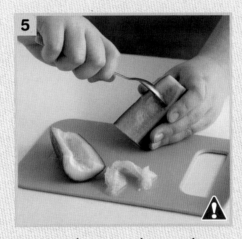

Remove the cucumber seeds using a teaspoon. Cut the cucumber, carrots, and peppers into equal strips – 24 in total.

6

Shiny side down

Put 1 sheet of nori on a bamboo mat. With wet hands, spread over ¼ of the rice. Add 6 vegetable strips as shown.

7

Tightly roll up the sushi using the bamboo mat. The nori naturally seals to itself when you reach the end.

8

Using a wet knife, trim the edges and cut into 6 slices. Repeat steps 6–8 to make the rest of the sushi rolls.

Sushi rolls are a popular dish globally, but they originated in Japan where Sotaro is from.

Jollof rice

This one-pot rice dish is coloured a red-orange by the juice from the tomatoes. It is popular in many West African countries.

YOU WILL NEED:
- 2 tbsp sunflower oil
- 1 large onion, chopped
- 1 clove garlic, crushed
- 400g (14oz) can chopped tomatoes
- 1 red pepper, deseeded and chopped
- 2 tbsp tomato purée
- salt and freshly ground black pepper
- 1 tsp chilli powder
- 1 tsp curry powder
- 1 bay leaf
- sprig fresh thyme
- 600ml (1pt) chicken or vegetable stock
- 225g (8oz) basmati or long-grain rice, rinsed under cold water
- 4 skinless, boneless chicken breasts

Heat 1 tablespoon of the oil in a pan. Cook the onions and garlic over a gentle heat for 4-5 minutes until soft.

Stir in the chopped tomatoes, red pepper, and tomato purée. Season with salt and pepper.

Add the chilli powder, curry powder, bay leaf, and thyme, then pour in the stock.

Bring to the boil, then reduce the heat. Cover and simmer for 5 minutes.

Add the rice. Bring to the boil. Reduce the heat to low. Cover and simmer for 25 minutes or until most of the liquid is absorbed.

Brush the chicken with the remaining oil. Griddle for 5-6 minutes on each side, until cooked through and golden.

TOP TIP
Serve with chicken or fish. For a vegetarian option, add a side of vegetables instead.

Jedidiah is from Ghana, where jollof rice is a traditional meal. It's often served with fried plantain.

Indian rice pudding

TOP TIP
Replace the pistachios with cashew nuts or almonds if you prefer.

In India, this dish is called "kheer" in the north and "payasam" in the south. There are many regional variations for this recipe, which can be eaten during a meal or as a dessert.

YOU WILL NEED:

- 100g (3½oz) basmati rice
- 750ml (1¼ pints) full-fat milk
- 3 tbsp caster sugar
- ½ tsp ground cardamom
- ½ tsp grated nutmeg
- 50g (1¾oz) sultanas or raisins
- 50g (1¾oz) pistachio nuts, chopped

1

Put the rice, milk, and sugar in a saucepan and bring to the boil. Reduce the heat and simmer for 10 minutes.

2

Stir in the cardamom, nutmeg, and sultanas. Reserve a few pistachios for decoration and stir in the rest.

3

Continue to cook over a low heat for a further 10 minutes, stirring often until the mixture is thick and creamy.

4

Spoon the rice into 4 serving dishes. Serve warm or cover and chill in the fridge to serve cold later on.

Vishnu is from India, where rice pudding is incredibly popular.

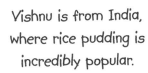

5

Before serving, decorate with the reserved pistachio nuts.

WHEAT

This bristly grass is one of the most important edible plants in the world. It's a staple food for billions of people and is grown almost everywhere. Wheat grains are ground into flour and used to make foods from cakes and pastries, to bread and pasta.

Wheat is a staple food for more than **35%** of the world's population.

Grains of wheat have been found in Ancient Egyptian **TOMBS.**

Wheat fields take up more **LAND** than any other crop.

Today, it takes less than **10 SECONDS** to harvest enough wheat for **70 BREAD LOAVES.**

Wheat and barley were the first grain crops to **EVER** be farmed.

People in Italy eat more than **23**kg **(50**lbs**)** of pasta per year.

HUGE HARVEST

People used to cut down wheat crops using sharp knives. Now they use a combine harvester. A combine can chop down 0.4 hectares (1 acre) of wheat in 6 minutes. That would take a person half a day!

Wheat crops are ready to harvest when they turn bright yellow.

China produces and eats the most wheat.

Growing WHEAT

Wheat is easy to grow and can be found all over the world – in high and low areas, and in hot and cold places. No matter what month it is, wheat is being harvested somewhere in the world.

Mighty machine

A combine harvester does many tasks at once. It **reaps** (cuts down the wheat crop), **threshes** (separates stalks from spikelets), and **winnows** (separates grains from chaff). It also **stores** grains in a tank.

Wheat plant

The spike (head) of the plant is made up of little spikelets.

A spikelet contains wheat grains, which are encased in chaff.

Stalk

Chaff

Leaf

Grain

Each spike of wheat has 40-60 grains!

ADAPTABLE GRASS

Today's wheat gives more grains and is more resistant to disease than ever before. Wheat stalks are also shorter than 100 years ago, as it's easier to harvest short, upright plants that don't bend over.

What's next?

The wheat grains are taken to a factory, where they're poured into machines, ready for processing. Most grains are then milled (ground down) into flour.

Types of wheat

When it's growing in the fields, wheat looks like bristly grass. However, by the time it's milled into flour or semolina, it looks completely different.

Early wheat

Wild varieties, such as "einkorn" and "emmer" grew more than 9,000 years ago. Over time, people grew types with more grains that clung to the stalks, making them easier to harvest.

People used to grind wheat by rolling a big stone over a flat stone. Phew!

Einkorn

Emmer

Common wheat

This is the most widely grown wheat species today. More than 90 per cent of all wheat is common wheat.

Common wheat grains

Common wheat

You can also eat wheat grains raw.

Durum wheat

Durum wheat is a special type of wheat that is very hard. This means it keeps its shape when it's cooked.

Durum grains

Durum wheat

Wheat to semolina

Durum wheat is ground down into coarse semolina. This is used to make couscous, grits, and pasta.

Semolina is mixed with water (or eggs) to make a dough. It's rolled out, cut into pasta shapes, and then left to dry.

Semolina

Pasta shapes

Common wheat is too soft to make into pasta – the shapes would fall apart when cooked.

Wheat to flour

Wheat grains are often milled into flour. There are many types of flour, which differ depending on which part of the wheat grain is used.

White flour is made from only part of the wheat grain.

Wholemeal flour is made from all of the wheat grain.

White self-raising flour

Light brown wholemeal flour

Plain white flour

Flour power!

Bread is made by combining flour with other ingredients, including water and yeast. There are all sorts of bread recipes around the world.

Bread can also be made from rice, maize, and potato flour.

A common Indian bread.

Popular in the Middle East.

Roti

Baguettes

Sliced, brown bread

Pitta

Doughnuts, USA

Doughnuts are deep-fried pastries. They are popular worldwide, but more than 10 BILLION are eaten in the USA every year!

Isn't it amazing that all these different dishes were made from the same base ingredient? Wheat is so versatile, it's used in staple meals, snacks, and sweet treats.

Solal, aged 7, France

Wonderful

Quiche Lorraine, France

Quiches are deep tarts. The outer pastry is made from wheat, and then it's filled with savoury custard and yummy extras, such as bacon and eggs.

Bassma, aged 8, Morocco

Couscous, Morocco

It may look like fluffy rice, but couscous is made from balls of semolina – a flour made from durum wheat. Couscous dishes often include meat, spices, and vegetables.

Noodle soup, China

Noodles are usually made from rice or wheat. Wheat noodles are used in this Chinese soup, which is popular all over Asia.

WHEAT

Lasagne, Italy

Durum wheat is used to make pasta, including flat lasagne sheets. The sheets are layered between sauces and fillings, and then it's all baked in an oven.

Martyna, aged 10, Poland

Apple cake, Poland

Traditional Polish apple cakes are made from a sweet pastry and have a spiced apple filling.

Khurrshuur, Mongolia

Dumplings wrap up other foods. For khurrshuur, the inside surprise is usually meat or potatoes.

Robert, aged 9, Mongolia

wholemeal bread roll

Clara and Lucy, aged 9, Australia

Anzac biscuits, Australia

Named after the Australian and New Zealand Army Corps (ANZAC), these biscuits were once hard and savoury, but now are sweet and often flavoured with coconut.

Four ways with pasta

Durum wheat is used to make more than 350 types of pasta. Follow the instructions to make a basic pasta, then choose from four of these delicious sauce recipes.

Bring slightly salted water to the boil in a large saucepan. Add the dried pasta and cook for 10-12 minutes.

Drain the pasta in a colander, then stir the pasta into the sauce.

Bolognese sauce

- 1 tbsp olive oil
- 1 onion, chopped
- 1 clove garlic, crushed
- 1 carrot, diced
- 1lb (450g) minced beef
- 150ml (¼pt) beef stock
- 400g (14oz) can chopped tomatoes
- 2 tbsp tomato purée
- 2 tsp dried mixed herbs

1. Heat the oil in a pan and add the onion, garlic, and carrot. Cook over a medium heat for 4-5 minutes until softened. **2.** Add the beef and cook until browned. Stir in the stock, tomatoes, purée, and herbs. Bring to the boil. **3.** Reduce the heat, cover, and simmer for 15 minutes until thickened.

Vegetable pasta sauce

- 1 small red onion, cut into 8 wedges
- 1 red pepper, and 1 yellow pepper, deseeded and chopped
- 1 courgette, chopped
- 1 clove garlic, crushed
- 2 tbsp olive oil
- 200ml (7fl oz) passata (or chopped tomatoes)
- handful fresh basil, torn
- salt

1. Mix the vegetables, garlic, and olive oil in a bowl. **2.** Heat a large griddle pan. Add the vegetables and cook for 3 minutes, turning occasionally, until lightly charred. **3.** Place in a large saucepan. Stir in the passata and bring to the boil. Simmer for 5 minutes. Stir in the basil and season to taste.

Four cheese sauce

- 2 tbsp softened butter
- 2 tbsp plain flour
- 125ml (4½fl oz) milk
- 75g (2½oz) grated mature Cheddar cheese
- 4 tbsp finely grated Parmesan cheese
- 75g (2½oz) soft cream cheese
- 75g (2½oz) mild blue cheese, crumbled
- salt and freshly ground black pepper

1. Place the butter, flour, and milk in a pan. Cook over a medium heat, whisking non-stop, until the mixture is smooth and thick. **2.** Remove from heat and stir in the cheeses. Place over a low heat and cook, stirring non-stop until the cheese melts. Season to taste.

Pesto sauce

- 50g (1¾oz) pine nuts
- 2 cloves garlic, chopped
- 1 tsp sea salt
- 50g (1¾oz) fresh basil leaves
- 125g (4½oz) fresh Parmesan cheese, grated
- 150ml (5fl oz) extra virgin olive oil

1. Place the pine nuts in a frying pan. Lightly toast for 2-3 minutes over a medium heat. **2.** Blitz the nuts, garlic, salt, and basil leaves in a food processor. Transfer to a bowl, then stir in the cheese. Slowly beat in the oil. **3.** To store, place the pesto in a storage jar and cover with olive oil. Keep in the fridge for up to week.

Vegetable chow mein

This Chinese meal shows off classic Asian flavours, such as ginger, soy sauce, and sesame oil. Serve this dish as a vegetarian main course or add meat or fish to boost the level of protein.

YOU WILL NEED:

- 225g (8oz) dried medium egg noodles

- 1 tbsp sunflower oil

- 1 clove garlic, crushed

- 1 tsp freshly grated root ginger

- 4 spring onions, sliced

- 2 carrots, peeled and cut into thin strips

- 125g (4½oz) shitake mushrooms, sliced

- 100g (3½oz) mangetout

- 2 tbsp light soy sauce

- 2 tbsp oyster sauce

- ½ tsp toasted sesame oil

- 100g (3½oz) beansprouts

This tasty meal is from China, where Shaowei lives. It's also a popular dish around the world.

1

Place the noodles in a pan of boiling water and simmer for 4 minutes.

2

Drain well, then return the noodles to the pan to keep them warm.

3

Heat the sunflower oil in a wok and add the garlic, ginger, and spring onions. Stir-fry for 2-3 minutes.

4

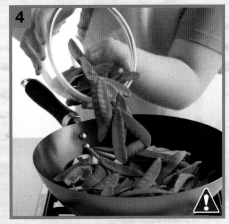

Add the carrots, mushrooms, and mangetout. Cook for a further 2-3 minutes.

5

In a bowl, mix together the soy sauce, oyster sauce, and sesame oil.

6

Add the beansprouts, noodles, and sauce. Make sure everything is coated with the sauce. Cook for 2-3 minutes.

Four ways with pizza

It's really easy to make your own pizza. Just follow the recipe for pizza dough, cover with sauce, and add your chosen toppings.

YOU WILL NEED:

• 225g (8oz) strong plain white flour, plus extra for dusting

• ½ tsp salt

• ½ tsp fast-action dried yeast

• 150ml (5fl oz) warm water

• 1 tbsp extra virgin olive oil

Put the flour, salt, and yeast in a large mixing bowl. Make a well in the centre. Stir in the water and oil to form a dough.

Place the dough on a lightly floured surface and knead for 7-10 minutes until smooth and stretchy.

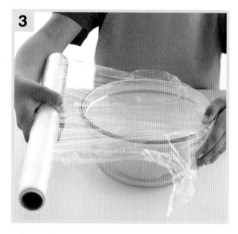

Place the dough in a lightly oiled bowl. Cover with cling film. Leave to rise in a warm place for 1 hour, or until doubled in size.

Preheat the oven to 220°C (425°F/Gas 7). Lightly oil a pizza tray.

Punch the dough to knock out air bubbles. Knead on a floured surface. Roll the dough out into a 30cm (12in) circle.

Put the dough on the pizza tray, then add sauces and toppings. See right for topping ideas and baking times.

Alsatian tarte flambée

- 200g (7oz) quark or fromage blanc
- 100g (3½oz) crème fraîche
- ½ tsp ground nutmeg
- 125g (4½oz) smoked streaky bacon, thinly sliced
- 1 onion, thinly sliced

Mix the quark with the crème fraîche and nutmeg. Spread over the pizza, then top with the bacon and onion. Cook for 10-12 minutes.

Margherita

- 6 tbsp pizza sauce
- 25g (1oz) grated mozzarella cheese
- 250g (9oz) pack mozzarella, drained and sliced
- 2 tomatoes, sliced
- fresh basil leaves

Spread the sauce over the pizza. Sprinkle over the grated cheese. Add the sliced mozzarella and tomatoes. Cook for 10-15 minutes. Garnish with the basil leaves.

Florentine

- 6 tbsp pizza sauce
- 50g (1¾oz) grated mozzarella cheese
- 225g (8oz) spinach leaves, cooked
- 50g (1¾oz) mozzarella ball, torn
- 4 eggs

Spread the sauce over the pizza. Add the grated cheese, spinach, and the torn mozzarella. Cook for 8 minutes. Crack over the eggs. Cook for 3-4 more minutes.

Hawaiian

- 50g (1¾oz) ham, chopped
- 3 pineapple rings, from a can, chopped
- 6 tbsp pizza sauce
- 85g (3oz) grated mozzarella cheese
- 50g (1¾oz) mozzarella ball, torn

Spread the sauce over the pizza, then add the cheese, ham, and pineapple. Cook for 10-12 minutes.

Gingerbread biscuits

Gingerbread tastes great and makes the house smell wonderful as it bakes. This recipe can be used for biscuits, pretty decorations, or gingerbread people.

TOP TIP
Allow the gingerbread biscuits to cool on the trays before taking them off.

Makes 15 • **45 mins** • **15 mins**

YOU WILL NEED:

- 2 large baking trays, lined with baking paper
- 125g (4½oz) unsalted butter, diced
- 100g (3½oz) soft dark brown sugar
- 4 tbsp golden syrup
- 1 tsp bicarbonate of soda
- 325g (11oz) plain flour, plus extra for dusting
- 2 tsp ground ginger
- ½ tsp ground cloves
- ½ tsp ground nutmeg
- ½ tsp ground cinammon

FOR THE ICING:

- 250g (9oz) icing sugar
- 2 tbsp water

TO DECORATE:

- Sugar sprinkles

Clara is 9 years old and lives in Germany, where gingerbread is sold at festive winter markets.

1

Melt the butter, sugar, and syrup in a pan over a low heat until the butter and sugar have dissolved. Set aside to cool.

2

Sift the bicarbonate of soda, flour, and spices into a large bowl and stir together.

3

Pour over the syrup and use a wooden spoon to mix well, until you have a soft, slightly sticky dough.

4

Wrap the dough in cling film and chill in the fridge for 30 minutes. Preheat the oven to 180°C (350°F/Gas 4).

5

Roll out the dough on a floured surface to a depth of 5mm (¼in). Cut out shapes and put on trays. Bake for 9 minutes.

6

Decorate the biscuits.

Sift the icing sugar into a bowl. Add the water a little at a time until you have a spreading consistency.

MAIZE

Millions of people rely on maize (also called corn) for the main part of their diet. Maize is often cooked and eaten on the cob, but it can also be popped, boiled, roasted, ground into flour, or grilled. People use maize to feed livestock and even to provide fuel for transport.

CHICKENS that eat a lot of maize have slightly **YELLOW** skin.

Maize is one of the ingredients used to make **chewing gum.**

There are more than **3,500** uses for maize products.

On average, a cob of maize has **800** kernels in **16 ROWS.**

Maize is used to sweeten **SOFT DRINKS.**

HUSKS from maize are used by Native Americans to make mats and baskets.

GROWING TALL

Maize is harvested during different months depending on what it will be used for. The later the maize is harvested, the drier the kernels will be.

The USA grows the most maize in the world.

Maize can grow up to 3.5m (12ft) high.

Growing MAIZE

Maize is one of the most useful and versatile crops in the world. It's a domesticated grass, which means it doesn't grow in the wild. Maize is grown on every continent, except Antarctica.

Maize plants

Maize is grown in fields in large quantities. Seeds are planted in moist and rich soil. It takes between 2-3 months from planting the seeds to harvesting. Maize needs warm weather to grow. It's sensitive to frost, so if it's planted too early an entire crop can be lost.

Maize plant

Silks

Kernels are attached to a central cob.

Husk

Kernels

Cobs always have an even number of rows of kernels.

Up until the 1930s, maize was mostly harvested by hand.

Harvest time

If maize is being eaten as a vegetable it's picked when the silks are green. However, if it's grown as a grain, it's picked when the silks are brown. Maize is usually harvested by a machine called a mechanical corn picker.

Types of maize

Maize comes in many colours and sizes. If it's picked early, maize is eaten as a vegetable, but if it's picked when it's fully grown, maize is used as a grain.

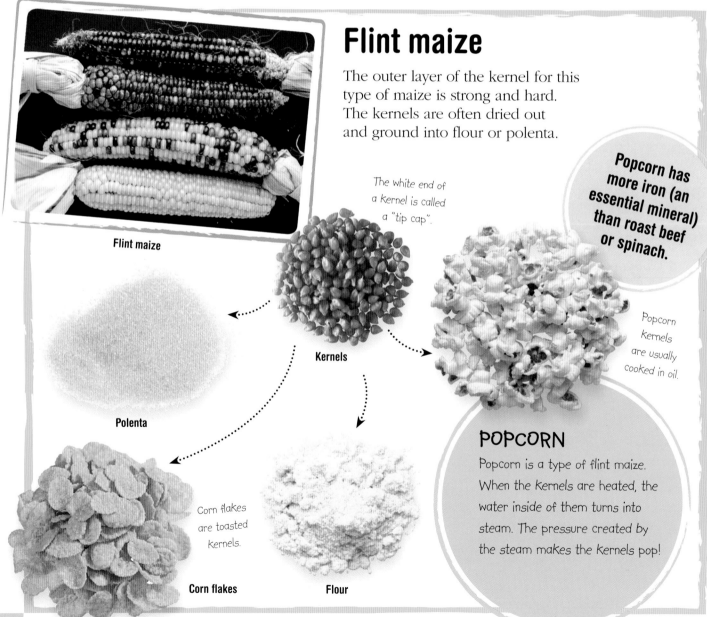

Flint maize

Flint maize

The outer layer of the kernel for this type of maize is strong and hard. The kernels are often dried out and ground into flour or polenta.

The white end of a kernel is called a "tip cap".

Popcorn has more iron (an essential mineral) than roast beef or spinach.

Kernels

Popcorn kernels are usually cooked in oil.

Polenta

POPCORN

Popcorn is a type of flint maize. When the kernels are heated, the water inside of them turns into steam. The pressure created by the steam makes the kernels pop!

Corn flakes are toasted kernels.

Corn flakes

Flour

Baby corn is maize that's harvested early.

Baby corn is eaten raw or cooked. It's picked from the plant before the stalks are fully grown.

Baby corn

STREET FOOD

Maize was first grown 9,000 years ago, in the place that is now Mexico. It's still popular there today, especially when it's heated and eaten directly off the cob.

Flour maize

Flour maize is usually used in baked food items. It comes in lots of colours including yellow, red, blue, black, and multi-colour.

These are made from a blue variety of flour maize.

Flour maize

Corn chips

Flour maize

Corn flour

These tacos are made from corn flour.

Corn chips

Tacos

Dent maize

Dent maize is also called "field corn". Dents form as the kernels dry. It's used for animal feed, to make plastic, and to create fuel.

Dents

Dent maize

Sweet maize

Sweet maize is usually called "sweet corn". It's grown to be eaten as a vegetable as it's harvested early when the kernels are soft and tender.

Sweet corn is usually tinned or frozen to keep it fresh.

Pod maize is an unusual variety as each kernel is encased in its own husk!

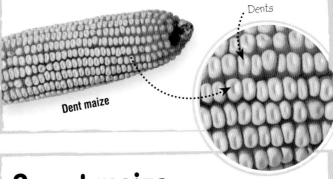

Tinned sweet corn

One of the best things about maize is that it can be used to make many delicious meals. This is one of the reasons so many countries have a famous dish that uses maize as the main ingredient.

Yohanna,
aged 7,
Ethiopia

Amazing

Popcorn, Ethiopia

Popcorn is traditionally served as part of an Ethiopian coffee ceremony. The coffee is prepared carefully as it's brewed three times.

Tamales, Mexico

This Mexican street food contains a sweet or savoury filling, wrapped in a "masa" dough and then steamed in a maize husk. The husk is discarded before eating.

Andrea, aged 7,
South Carolina, USA

Grits, USA

Hard, dried maize kernels are ground down to make grits. This porridge-like mash is often served as part of a meal, or has prawns and bacon on top.

46

Sweet corn fritters, Thailand

A batter is made from flour, corn, egg, spring onions, and coriander. The batter is fried in oil until golden and served with a sweet chilli dip.

Cymian, aged 10, Montana, USA

CORN

Corn on the cob, USA

This is a popular side dish worldwide. It's often served with melted butter on top. Historically, Native Americans ate corn that was boiled or roasted.

Sweetcorn chowder, Jamaica

Creamy and tasty, the base for this soup is coconut milk. It's on the spicy side because it has chillies and cayenne pepper.

sweet corn Kernels

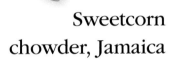

Shigo, aged 7, Tanzania

Grilled polenta, Italy

To make polenta, maize is ground into a flour and mixed with oil, salt, and water in a saucepan. It's then poured into a dish and grilled in an oven.

Ugali, Tanzania

Ugali is made from maize flour and is cooked in boiling liquid. It's a bit like porridge, and is a staple dish in parts of Africa.

Chicken fajitas

Serve this lightly spiced chicken and vegetable dish on corn tortillas, which are thin, unleavened flat breads, made from finely ground maize.

Alonso is from Mexico. "Tex-mex" cuisine (such as fajitas) is a fusion of Texan and Mexican food.

TOP TIP
You can add other ingredients to your tortillas, such as grated Cheddar cheese.

YOU WILL NEED:

- 450g (1lb) skinless, boneless chicken breasts, cut into thin strips

- 1 red pepper, deseeded and sliced

- 1 yellow pepper, deseeded and sliced

- 1 red onion, sliced

- 1 tsp smoked paprika

- 1 tsp ground cumin

- 1 tsp mild chilli powder

- 1 tsp dried oregano

- 1 lime

- 1 tbsp sunflower oil

- ½ tsp freshly ground black pepper

TO SERVE:

- 8 corn tortillas

- tomato salsa

- soured cream

- guacamole

1

Place the chicken, peppers, and onion in a large bowl, add all the spices.

2

Finely grate the zest from the lime rind. Use a hand-held juicer to squeeze all the juice from the lime.

3

Add the lime zest and juice, the seasoning, and 1 teaspoon of the oil. Stir well to coat the vegetables and chicken.

4

Heat the remaining oil in a frying pan. Add the chicken mixture and cook for 6-8 minutes, until cooked through.

5

Warm the corn tortillas according to pack instructions. Add the chicken, salsa, soured cream, and guacamole.

6

Fold the tortilla over or roll up and serve immediately.

Cornbread

This recipe is really simple to make. The spring onions give it an interesting texture and taste. It's best served warm and is perfect for a healthy snack or as a side dish.

YOU WILL NEED:

- 20cm (8in) square cake tin
- Butter to grease tin
- 1 tbsp baking powder
- 250g (9oz) coarse cornmeal (polenta)
- 5 spring onions, finely chopped
- 1 tsp salt
- 2 large eggs
- 300ml (10fl oz) buttermilk (or milk or plain yogurt with a squeeze of lemon juice)
- 50g (1¾oz) butter, melted and cooled

Butter the square cake tin. Line the base with baking paper. Preheat the oven to 200°C (400°F/Gas 6).

In a large bowl, add the baking powder, cornmeal, spring onions, and salt. Mix well with a wooden spoon.

Put the eggs, buttermilk, and melted butter in a measuring jug and mix together.

Pour the egg mixture into the dry ingredients and stir well to combine everything.

Pour and then smooth the mixture in the tin. Bake for 25-30 minutes until golden.

Allow to cool in the tin for 10 minutes, then turn out. Remove the baking paper and cut into 24 squares.

TOP TIP
Any remaining cornbread can be stored in a tin for up to 2 days.

Cornbread is popular in the USA, where Lily is from. She lives in a state called Ohio.

POTATOES

More than one billion people regularly eat potatoes. They were once only grown in the mountains of South America, but are now the most widely grown, non-grass crop in the world. Throughout history, potatoes have been a huge part of people's diets, especially as they're so versatile, and full of filling carbohydrates.

More than **380 MILLION** tonnes (420 million tons) of potatoes are grown per year.

POTATOES and **TOMATOES** come from the same plant family.

Pictures of potatoes can be seen on ancient South American **POTTERY.**

The average potato is made up of **80%** water.

Too much light makes potatoes turn **GREEN.**

The Inca people who lived long ago measured **TIME** by how long it took to cook a potato.

POTATO PLANTING

On a farm, a farmer ploughs the land, removing any stones that may get in the potatoes' way. Seed potatoes are then planted far apart in rows using a potato planting machine.

Potato production has grown in ASIA and AFRICA because of INVESTMENT, RESEARCH, and new growing TECHNOLOGIES.

Growing POTATOES

Potatoes are a successful crop because they are easy to grow, transport, and sell. In the past 50 years, production has increased more than any other crop, especially in Asia and Africa.

A sprouting seed potato

Shoots sprout from a potato's "eyes."

SEED START

Potatoes are grown from other potatoes, called "seed potatoes." Seed potatoes ensure all potatoes grown will be exactly the same type.

Potato plant

Leaves

Stem

Seed potato

Developing tuber

Roots

Fully-grown potato

Growing underground

The potatoes we eat are the underground "tubers" of the potato plant. Tubers are the enlarged parts of the plant's stem. They grow under the soil, and get all their nutrients from the plant above.

DEADLY DISEASE

Blight is a disease that destroys potato crops. It caused crop failure all over Europe in the 1800s.

> Potatoes grow in both high and low, and hot and cold places.

Ready to pick

Potatoes are ready to be dug up when the plant leaves start to wither. A harvester lifts potatoes out from the soil. Any dirt and soil are then removed before they are taken to a factory.

Potatoes are...

☑ full of minerals (when the skin's left on)

☑ a good source of Vitamin C

Types of potato

There are more than 4,500 types of potatoes. They vary in colour, and can look like teeny tiny balls, big bulky rocks, or even knobbly fingers!

Potatoes are used to make crisps, a popular snack worldwide.

The most nutritious part of a potato is just inside the skin.

Waxy

Some potatoes have waxy skins. This means their skin stays on when cooked, so they're best when boiled and steamed.

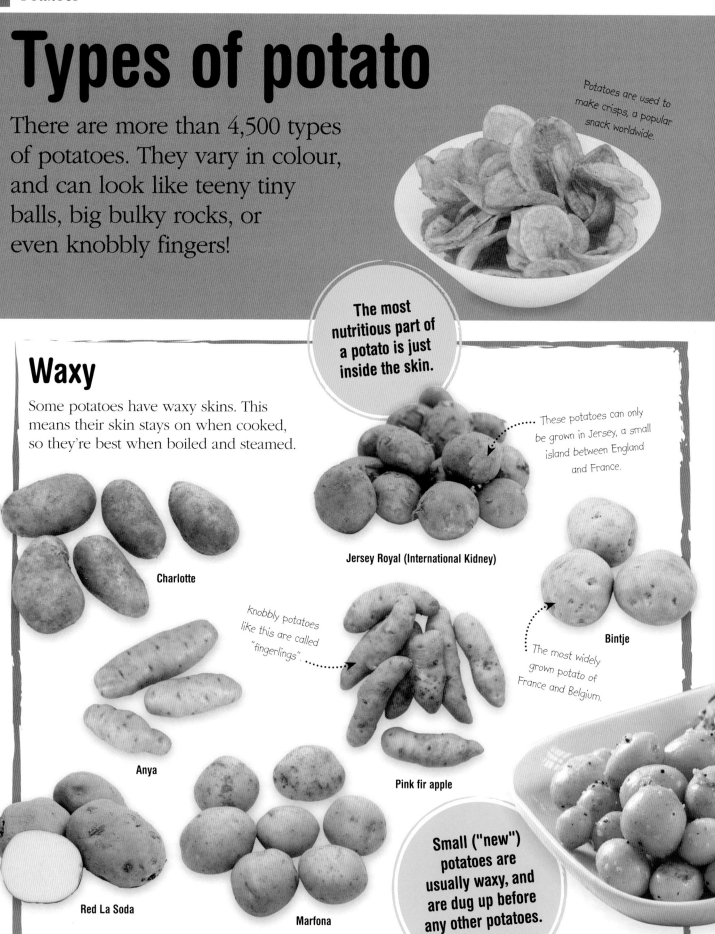

These potatoes can only be grown in Jersey, a small island between England and France.

Jersey Royal (International Kidney)

Charlotte

knobbly potatoes like this are called "fingerlings".

Bintje

The most widely grown potato of France and Belgium.

Anya

Pink fir apple

Red La Soda

Marfona

Small ("new") potatoes are usually waxy, and are dug up before any other potatoes.

FREEZE-DRIED

In South America, potatoes are laid out in fields. There they are frozen at night and are bleached by the Sun in the day. People also stomp on them with bare feet to get rid of any excess liquid. This creates a long-lasting product called chuño.

Potatoes high in starch are ideal for making fluffy, mashed potatoes.

Starchy

Other potatoes have floury, starchy skins. This means their skin falls off when cooked. They're better baked, roasted, and mashed.

Some potatoes are purple!

Vitelotte

Arran Victory

King Edward

Russet

Maris Piper

Chips

Starchy potatoes make great chips and fries.

All-purpose

These potatoes have a medium amount of starch, meaning they fall inbetween starchy and waxy potatoes.

Purple Majesty

Yukon Gold

Rooster

Desirée

Accent

You can use all-purpose potatoes to make baked potatoes.

Boil them, fry them, mash them... there are so many things you can do with potatoes. They're great to accompany a main meal, and are equally delicious when they take centre stage.

Rösti, Switzerland

Swiss-German farmers originally ate rösti for breakfast, but now it's a common side dish. The potatoes are grated, shaped into circles, and fried in oil until crispy.

Perfect

boiled new potatoes

Cottage pie, UK

Poor people who lived in small houses (called cottages) first ate this dish. It has a mashed potato topping and minced beef inside.

Aloo gobi, India

In North India, potatoes ("aloo") and cauliflower ("gobi") are often cooked together. This dish is sometimes called aloo gobi in restaurants.

Mehak, aged 8, India

Llapingacho, Ecuador

A recipe from the Andes mountains, the potatoes are mashed into a patty, filled with a soft cheese, and then fried. The meal is usually served with peanut sauce and sausages.

POTATOES

Olivier salad, Russia

Let's celebrate! In Russia and its neighbouring countries, children often eat potato salad at birthday parties.

Yaroslav, aged 8, Russia

Jack, aged 7, Ireland

Irish stew, Ireland

This one-pot dish contains potatoes, lamb, or mutton. It's a firm family favourite but has humble beginnings in rural Ireland.

Poutine, Canada

Poutine is a combination of chips, cheese curds, and gravy. It was voted one of the best Canadian inventions of all time!

Lauryn, aged 8, Canada

Tortilla española, Spain

Spanish omelettes are made from potatoes and eggs. They are popular as a snack, as tapas (a light meal), and in packed lunch boxes for school.

Baked potatoes

Baked potatoes can be eaten as either a side dish or as a main meal. In the UK, it's called a "jacket potato" because of the crispy skin. A variety of fillings are eaten with them. Here are four delicious options.

YOU WILL NEED:

• 4 baking or floury potatoes (e.g. Maris Pipers, King Edwards, Estimas, Desirees)

• 1 tbsp sunflower oil

• 1 tbsp coarse sea salt

1

Preheat the oven to 200°C (400°F/Gas 6). Prick each potato all over with a fork then brush all over with the oil.

2

Put the salt on a shallow plate. Roll each potato in the salt and then place on a baking tray.

3

Cook for 1 hour or until the skin is crisp. Cut a cross in the top of each one and squeeze apart. Top with your choice of filling.

Chilli con carne

• 1 tsp sunflower oil
• 1 small onion, chopped
• 300g (10oz) lean minced beef or turkey
• 1-2 tsp chilli powder, to taste

• 1 tsp ground cumin
• 400g (14oz) can chopped tomatoes
• 1 tbsp tomato ketchup
• 400g (14oz) can red kidney beans, drained

1. Heat the oil in a frying pan and add the onion and mince. Cook over a medium heat for 3-4 minutes, until browned. Stir in the spices, tomatoes, ketchup, and beans. **2.** Bring to the boil, then simmer for 10 minutes, until thickened. Spoon onto the potatoes.

Bacon and pineapple

- 8 streaky smoked bacon rashers
- 75g (2½oz) cream cheese
- 4 pineapple rings, from a can, drained and chopped
- freshly ground black pepper

1. Dry-fry the bacon in a frying pan over a medium heat for 2-3 minutes each side until crispy, then remove and drain on kitchen paper. **2.** Place the cheese in a small bowl and beat until softened, then stir in the pineapple and season. Break the bacon into small pieces. Spoon the pineapple mixture over the potatoes and sprinkle with the crispy bacon.

Baked beans and cheese

- 2 x 400g (14oz) cans baked beans
- 75g (2½oz) grated Cheddar cheese

Reheat the beans according to the instructions on the can, then spoon over the potatoes. Sprinkle over a little cheese.

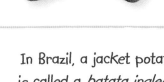

In Brazil, a jacket potato is called a *batata inglesa*, which means "English potato".

Tuna and sweet corn

- 2 x 160g (5¾oz) cans tuna chunks, in water or brine, drained
- 125g (4½oz) sweet corn from a can
- 4 tbsp mayonnaise
- 2 spring onions, chopped (optional)
- freshly ground black pepper

Place all the ingredients in a small bowl and mix together. Season to taste. Spoon onto the potatoes.

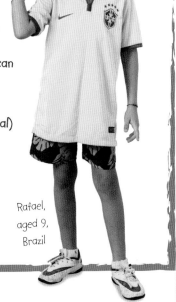

Rafael, aged 9, Brazil

Swedish hash

In Sweden, this dish is called *pyttipanna* meaning "teeny pieces in a pan". It's a great way of using up leftovers. The runny egg yolk makes a yummy topping.

TOP TIP
Use a non-stick frying pan to fry the potatoes and to avoid food sticking to the pan.

YOU WILL NEED:

- 25g (1oz) butter

- 2 tbsp sunflower oil

- 600g (1lb 5oz) potatoes, peeled and cut into 1cm (½in) cubes

- 2 onions, finely chopped

- 4 rashers smoked streaky bacon, chopped

- 400g (14oz) leftover roast meat (pork or beef), cut into 1cm (½in) cubes

- 2 frankfurters or smoked sausage, sliced

- 1 sprig fresh thyme, plus a few leaves for garnish

- Salt and freshly ground black pepper

- 4 eggs

Stella is from Sweden. This dish is popular in her country and in the countries nearby.

1 Heat the butter and 1 tbsp of the oil in a pan. When foaming, add the potatoes and onions. Fry for 15 minutes.

2 Cook the bacon in another pan over a medium heat. When the fat starts to run, add the meat and sausages.

3 Add the fresh thyme. Fry the mixture over a moderate heat for 4-5 minutes, stirring occasionally.

4 Add the meat mixture to the potatoes and onions and mix thoroughly. Season to taste.

5 Heat the leftover oil in the pan you used to cook the meat. Crack open the eggs, and add to pan. Fry for 3-4 minutes.

6 Serve the hash on plates, with a fried egg on the top of each one. Sprinkle over the remaining thyme leaves.

Other STAPLES around the world

When the four main staples are in short supply, difficult to buy, or impossible to grow, people look to other food sources. These "other staples" range from milk and cheese to root vegetables and legumes.

Dairy products are cheese, butter, cream, and yogurt.

Dairy

The animals shown below provide milk for people to drink. Their milk is also used to make dairy products, which contain lots of protein and calcium.

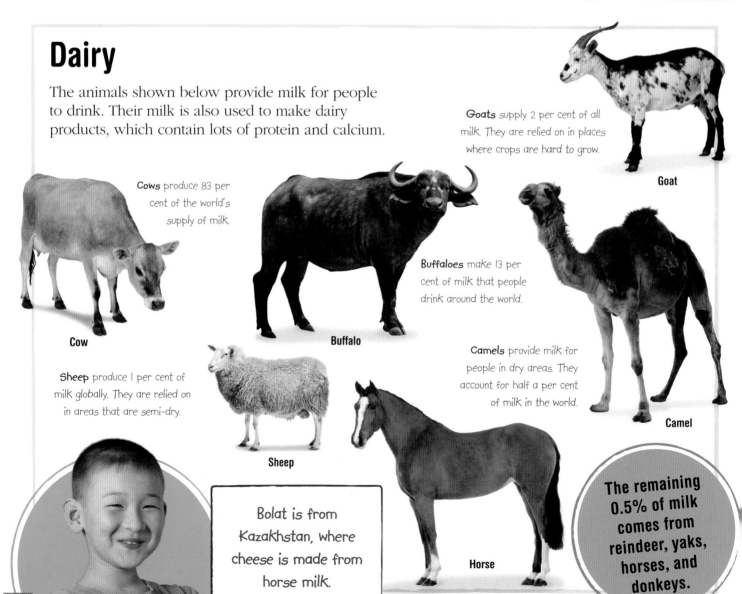

Goats supply 2 per cent of all milk. They are relied on in places where crops are hard to grow.

Goat

Cows produce 83 per cent of the world's supply of milk.

Cow

Buffaloes make 13 per cent of milk that people drink around the world.

Buffalo

Camels provide milk for people in dry areas. They account for half a per cent of milk in the world.

Camel

Sheep produce 1 per cent of milk globally. They are relied on in areas that are semi-dry.

Sheep

Bolat is from Kazakhstan, where cheese is made from horse milk.

Horse

The remaining 0.5% of milk comes from reindeer, yaks, horses, and donkeys.

Meat

Animal meat is eaten around the world because it's high in protein and provides lots of calories. Pork, poultry, and beef are eaten the most.

Poultry is the word used to describe meat derived from domestic birds, such as chickens, ducks, turkeys, and geese.

Chicken
Chicken meat is cheap to buy in most countries.

Turkey

Duck

Goose

Goat meat is lower in calories and fat than most other types of meat.

Goat

Reindeer

Mattus is from Finland, where reindeer meat is popular.

Lamb is the word for a baby sheep. It's eaten in lots of countries. Meat from an adult sheep is called mutton.

Sheep

Pork is meat that comes from pigs. There are more than 180 species of pig.

Pig

Beef is meat that comes from cows. The average cow weighs 545kg (1,200lbs).

Cow

People also eat meat from rabbits, deer, camels, and horses.

Fish

Fish and seafood are also a common source of animal protein. More than one billion people around the world eat fish as their main protein.

Tuna

Popular fish are carp, catfish, cod, eel, haddock, halibut, herring, mackerel, salmon, sardine, scad, snapper, trout, and tuna.

Salmon

China is the world's biggest fishing nation. They catch and farm more fish than any other country.

Mackerel

Tai is from Vietnam. Fish and seafood are staples there.

Root vegetables

Grown under the earth and in the soil, these vegetables are packed with nutrients and filling carbohydrates.

Rafael lives in Brazil, where cassava is grown and eaten a lot.

Taro is a staple food in Fiji and other Pacific Island countries.

Taro

Cassava

Some people call sweet potatoes "yams", but they are two completely different root vegetables.

Yam

Sweet potato

Fruit

Although many fruits are sweet, sugary snacks, some are starchy or full of fats. These fruits are staples in the warm countries where they're grown.

Avocados were a staple in central and southern America for thousands of years.

Avocado

Breadfruit

Jackfruit

Jackfruits and breadfruits are grown for their nutritious skins. Jackfruits are huge – they grow up to 90cm (36in) long!

Olives were once a staple food in Greece, where Maria lives.

Olives

Plantain

Legumes

These foods are full of fibre, and come from a family of plants called legumes. They grow on plants, and are encased in pods.

Murk comes from Pakistan. Lentil dishes called "dal" are popular there.

Soybeans are the most widely produced legume in the world.

Soybeans

Soybeans are highly nutritious. They are used to make soy milk, soy sauce, and tofu.

There are many varieties of lentils, and they vary in colour, from red and yellow to green and brown.

Lentils

Green peas

Chickpeas

Mung beans

Cowpeas
(black eyed peas)

Black-eyed peas grow really well in hot countries where it doesn't rain very much.

India produces almost 70% of the world's pigeon peas.

Beans are eaten with rice or samp (ground down maize kernels) in South Africa, where Amu lives.

Pigeon peas

Milk

More than 80 per cent of the world's **milk** supply comes from **cows**. Milk has more natural nutrients than any other drink. Cow's milk was first drunk by humans 10,000 years ago.

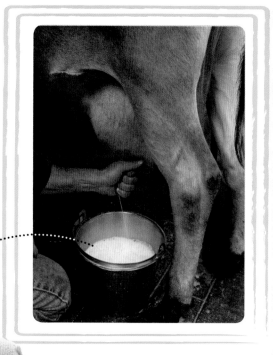

Milk is...

☑ full of calcium

☑ great for strong teeth and bones

Getting ready

Cow's milk goes through a process called pasteurisation, which gets rid of any harmful germs.

Milking machines

A cow is ready to be milked when her udders are full. Milking used to be done by hand, but milking machines are far faster, and can milk 24 cows at a time.

There are 1.5 BILLION cows in the world.

A cow makes enough MILK each day to fill 144 GLASSES.

Milk is used in pancakes. Crêpes (thin pancakes) are popular in France, where Morgan lives.

DAIRY PRODUCTS

About a quarter of all milk collected is used to make cheese. There are lots of different types of cheese. Milk is also used to make butter, yogurt, and ice cream.

Pancakes

Recipes and methods for making pancakes vary around the world. Try out this sweet version.

YOU WILL NEED:

- 20cm (8in) non-stick frying pan
- 100g (3½oz) plain flour
- pinch of salt
- 2 eggs, beaten
- 300ml (10fl oz) milk
- 2 tbsp melted butter
- sunflower oil, for frying

TO SERVE:

- 1 banana, thinly sliced
- chocolate sauce

TOP TIP
For a savoury dish, fill the pancake with grated cheese and ham instead.

1
Sift the flour and salt into a large bowl. Gradually whisk in the eggs. Then slowly whisk in the milk, until the batter is smooth. Stir in the melted butter.

2
Heat a little of the oil in the pan. Add a large spoonful of batter and swirl it around to create a thin, even layer. Cook for 1-2 minutes until golden.

3
Flip over and cook the other side for 1 minute. Remove from the pan. Make more pancakes with the remaining batter, adding extra oil if needed.

Chicken

Long ago, people didn't know how to grow crops, so the first staple foods were **meat**. **Chicken** is one of the most widely eaten meats in the whole world.

EXCELLENT EGGS

Chickens are bred to produce good quality meat and eggs. Female chickens are kept on farms to lay eggs. Ancient Egyptians had chicken farms more than 4,000 years ago!

Chicken is...

☑ high in Vitamin B6 (good for the immune system)

☑ a good source of calcium

Farm facts

People used to raise chickens at home. Today, most chickens live on huge farms. Free-range chickens have room to move around outside.

Benefits

Chicken is a great source of nutrition as it's packed with protein, vitamins and minerals, and it's low in fat. If you remove the skin before eating chicken, it reduces the fat content even more.

Egg cartons are cleverly shaped to protect eggs from cracking.

There are more than 19 BILLION chickens in the world.

In the UK, where Alec lives, people regularly eat roast chicken with vegetables and potatoes.

Chicken can be barbecued.

Roast chicken dinner

Kebabs

Try out these chicken kebabs or make a variety of your own using beef, lamb, or fish.

1

In a large bowl, mix the orange zest and juice, ginger, soy sauce, and honey. Season with pepper and mix together well.

2

Add the chicken and mix to coat, then leave to marinate for 1-2 hours.

3

Thread the vegetables and chicken onto the skewers. Preheat the grill to high and cook the kebabs for 12-15 minutes, turning once.

Sweet potatoes

Despite their name, **sweet potatoes** aren't potatoes, but one of the most eaten **root vegetables**. Often called a "superfood", they're a great source of energy, and also full of goodness.

Shoots are cut to become slips.

China produces most of the world's sweet potatoes.

SLIP GROWING

Most sweet potatoes are grown from "slips". These are the shoots that grow from a sweet potato. The shoots are cut off and left to grow their own roots, before being planted.

Sweet potatoes...

☑ are an excellent source of Vitamins A and C

☑ support your immune system

Sweet potatoes

Lots of land

Sweet potato plants are traditionally grown in warm countries, but can now be grown in colder places too. They take up a lot of space as they grow.

Sweet potatoes can be mashed, boiled, roasted, or fried.

Colourful crop

Sweet potatoes can be orange, brown, red, or purple. Orange sweet potatoes have more beta-carotene than other varieties. Beta-carotene supports healthy skin.

Sweet potato wedges

Perfect as a side dish or snack, these wedges are a tasty treat and packed with lots of nutrients.

TOP TIP
This snack is great with dips, such as soured cream or tomato sauce.

Preheat the oven to 200°C (400°F/Gas 6). Cut each potato into 8 wedges, then place in a large bowl.

Pour over the oil, then add the garlic, herbs, and seasoning. Mix well with a spoon to coat all the wedges.

Place the wedges on a non-stick tray in a single layer. Cook in the oven for 25-30 minutes (turning once), until golden and crispy.

YOU WILL NEED:

- 2 medium sweet potatoes, scrubbed
- 1 tbsp sunflower oil
- 2 cloves garlic, crushed
- 1 tsp dried thyme
- 1 tsp dried rosemary
- 1 tsp dried oregano
- salt and freshly ground black pepper

Plantains

Fruits that fill you up, such as avocados, breadfruit, and **plantains**, are a big part of people's diets. Plantains are closely related to bananas, but are more starchy and filling, and have thicker skins.

Growing plantains

Plantain plants aren't trees, but they can grow as tall as trees! Farmers prefer to grow them to a medium height, as taller ones get damaged by strong winds.

UGANDA produces the most plantains in the world.

Starchy staple

Plantains are a main source of carbohydrates for more than 70 million people. They are a staple food in African, Caribbean, and South and Central American countries.

Tostones

Ripe plantains are yellow with brown blotches.

Plantains start off green, and then turn yellow and finally black.

Black plantains are fine to eat, and very sweet inside.

TASTY TREATS

Green plantains are cooked in a similar way to potatoes. They are good for making plantain chips, such as the tostones, above.

Plantains are...

- ☑ high in fibre
- ☑ packed with potassium
- ☑ a good source of Vitamin C

Plantains are often grown and eaten in Colombia, where Miguel lives.

Plantain chips

These lightly spiced crisps are baked rather than fried, and taste great with a creamy dip.

TOP TIP
Allow the plantains to cool on the baking sheet for 5 minutes before serving.

YOU WILL NEED:

- 2 green plantains, peeled and cut into 5mm (¼in) thick slices
- 1 tbsp sunflower oil
- 1 tsp sea salt
- 1 tsp smoked paprika
- ½ tsp chilli powder
- ½ tsp ground cumin

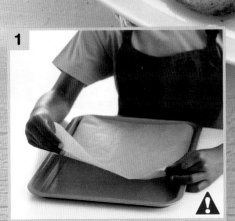

1 Preheat the oven to 200°C (400°F/ Gas 6). Line 2 large baking trays with baking paper.

2 Put the plantain slices in a bowl and mix in the oil, salt, and spices, until evenly coated. Place the slices on the baking paper.

3 Bake the slices for 15-20 minutes, until golden. Swap the trays over halfway through and flip the slices over.

Chickpeas

Legumes are a group of filling foods that include peas, beans, and lentils. **Chickpeas**, also known as garbanzo beans, are one of the most widely grown legume crops.

India GROWS, EATS, and IMPORTS the most chickpeas.

Pod power

Chickpeas grow in pods on small, bushy plants. It takes about 100 days until they're ready to be picked. Chickpeas start off bright green and gradually become paler.

Old goodness

Chickpeas are high in nutrients. They were one of the first legumes to be grown by people. We've grown them for 7,500 years!

Chickpeas are...

☑ packed with manganese (good for healthy bones)

☑ full of fibre

There are 1-2 chickpeas per pod.

Chickpeas are a good meat substitute as they're full of protein.

Chickpeas can be ground into flour.

MAKING MEALS

Some people eat chickpeas just as they are, but others use them in popular dishes, such as falafels or houmous.

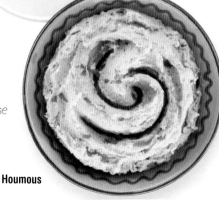

Houmous

YOU WILL NEED:

- 2 x 400g (14oz) cans chickpeas, drained well
- 2 garlic cloves, crushed
- 1 tbsp ground cumin
- 1 tsp ground coriander
- 1 tsp freshly ground black pepper
- 2 tbsp freshly chopped coriander
- 1 medium egg
- 2 tbsp toasted sesame seeds
- 1 tsp baking powder
- 1 tbsp oil, for frying

MINT DIP:

- 100g (3½oz) natural yogurt
- 2 tbsp freshly chopped mint
- ¼ cucumber, finely chopped

Falafels

This middle-eastern dish uses chickpeas as its main ingredient.

TOP TIP
Serve with toasted pitta bread, chopped tomatoes, and the mint dip.

Pulse the chickpeas, garlic, spices, pepper, and fresh coriander in a processor until coarsely chopped. Add the egg, seeds, and baking powder. Pulse again.

Roll the mixture into 16 balls, then flatten slightly. Chill for 30 minutes. Preheat the oven to 190°C (375°F/Gas 5).

Fry the falafels in the oil over a medium heat for 2-3 minutes each side. Place on a baking tray and bake for 10 minutes. Then mix up the dip in a bowl.

77

Equipment

It's important that you use the correct equipment for each task. Be careful with items that are sharp or require electricity to power them. Always have an adult present when you use them.

pasta spoon

wooden spatula

large plastic spoon

plastic spatula

wooden spoon

Kitchen basics

colander

set of plastic plates

oven gloves

cling film

fork

table knife

tea towels

salt and pepper grinders

set of small glass bowls

set of plastic bowls

tin opener

Frying, boiling, grilling, and stewing

grill pan

frying pans

wok

saucepan with lid

griddle pan

set of saucepans

Crushing, juicing, blending

garlic crusher

potato masher

food processor

hand-held juicer

Weighing, measuring

measuring cups

measuring jug

scales

tablespoon

teaspoon

Baking

cookie cutters

large glass bowl

cooling rack

whisk

baking tray

20cm (8in) square cake tin

pastry brush

sieves

pizza tray

rolling pin

icing piping bag

baking paper/ parchment

Cutting and chopping

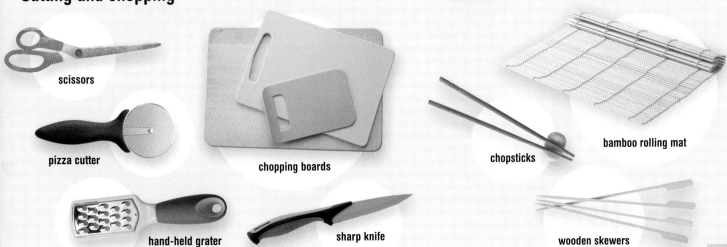

scissors

pizza cutter

chopping boards

hand-held grater

sharp knife

Extras

chopsticks

bamboo rolling mat

wooden skewers

INDEX

ACKNOWLEDGEMENTS

DK would like to say a massive **thank you** to all the children who first appeared in *Children Just Like Me (CJLM)* and extend our thanks to the CJLM team. We'd also like to thank the children's photographers – Idris Ahmed, Andy Crawford, Vinh Dao Karin Duthie, Mulugeta Gebrekidan, Alan Keohane, Mike Merchant, and James Tye.

The *Food Like Mine* team would also like to thank James Mitchem, Sarah Foakes, and Magenta Fox for editorial assistance, Sakshi Saluja for picture credits, Rachael Hare for illustrations, and Anne Damerell for legal assistance. We'd also like to give a special thanks to our wonderful hand models: Anushka Campbell-Butler, NaZia Gifford, Jena Robb, Dylan Tannazi, and Skylar Thunberg.

The publisher would like to thank the following for their kind permission to reproduce their photographs:

(Key: a-above; b-below/bottom; c-centre; f-far; l-left; r-right; t-top)

2-3 123RF.com: Oleg Doroshin (b). **3 123RF.com:** Feng Yu (ca); Natika (cl). **5 Dreamstime.com:** Eric Isselee (cla). **6 123RF.com:** Gilberto Mevi (c). **8 123RF.com:** Kitchakron sonnoy (clb); Photoroad (cra); Oleksii Olkin (crb). **Getty Images:** Andy Sacks (cla). **10-11 123RF.com:** Kitchakron sonnoy. **12 123RF.com:** Aliaksandr Mazurkevich (t). **13 123RF. com:** creativesunday (fcr); Thanyani Srisombut (tl); Nontawat Thongsibsong (tr); Varandah (cl); Kittiphat Inthonprasit (cr). **Getty Images:** Enrique Soriano / Bloomberg (clb). **14 123RF.com:** design56 (br); Jatesada Natayo (cra); Solomonjee (cl); Junghwa You (c); Kevin Brine (bl). **15 123RF.com:** amylv (cr); Heinz tschanz-hofmann (tr); jirkaejc (ca); Fabrizio Troiani (bc). **16 123RF.com:** redhayabusa (cra). **iStockphoto.com:** pop_jop (tr, ca, c, crb). **17 Dreamstime.com:** Vtupinamba (br). **iStockphoto. com:** pop_jop (tc, tr, c, clb, cb). **24-25 Getty Images:** Andy Sacks. **26 123RF.com:** Katerina Skokanova (t). **27 123RF.com:** Natika (cb). **Alamy Stock Photo:** omphoto (cl). **iStockphoto. com:** Jovanjaric (crb). **28 123RF.com:** Francesco Dibartolo (cra). **29 123RF.com:** Martinak (cr). **30 123RF.com:** cokemomo (br).

iStockphoto.com: pop_jop (tc, ca, cb, crb). **31 123RF.com:** mors74 (c). **iStockphoto.com:** pop_jop (tl, ca, cr, cb). **40-41 123RF.com:** Photoroad. **42 123RF.com:** Shvadchak Vasyl (t). **43 123RF.com:** Steven Heap (cb). **Dreamstime.com:** Megalomaniac (cla). **44 123RF.com:** Arinahabich (cl); Hamsterman (bl). **45 123RF.com:** Bohuslav Jelen (c); yelo34 (tr); Kumruen Pakorn (cl); ildipapp (fclb); Yana Gayvoronskaya (clb); Sergey Skleznev (cb); Diana Taliun (bl); Svitlana Symonova (br). **Alamy Stock Photo:** Greg Wright (cr). **46 iStockphoto.com:** pop_jop (ca, cl, cb). **47 iStockphoto.com:** pop_jop (tr, ca, cr, cb, crb). **52-53 123RF.com:** Oleksii Olkin. **54 123RF.com:** Wilaiwan Jantra (t). **54-55 123RF.com:** Oleg Doroshin (b). **55 123RF.com:** Jakub Janele (clb); Pavel Rodimov (cla); lilkar (c); Leblond Catherine (cra). **57 123RF.com:** Denisfilm (bc); Feng Yu (clb). **Alamy Stock Photo:** Keith Leighton (c); Nacho Calonge (cr). **58 123RF.com:** Alexander Mychko (clb); Pablo Hidalgo (bc). **iStockphoto.com:** pop_jop (tr, ca, clb/Flag, cb). **58-59 123RF. com:** Yana Gayvoronskaya. **59 123RF.com:** vvoennyy (ftl). **iStockphoto.com:** pop_jop (tl, ca, cb, crb). **64 123RF.com:** Bennymarty (c); Eric Isselee (cr, br). **65 Dreamstime.com:** Eric Isselee (cr). **66 123RF.com:** Chatuphot Chatchawan (crb); Napat Polchoke (crb/Cut Jackfruit). **67 123RF.com:** Handmadepictures (cr); Joannawnuk (cla); Riccardo Motti (clb); PhotosIndia.com LLC (bc). **68 123RF.com:** Baloncici (c). **70 iStockphoto.com:** pop_jop

(cb). **72 123RF.com:** Suwit Gaewsee-ngam (cla). **Dorling Kindersley:** Moss Doerksen (cl). **74 123RF.com:** Chad Zuber (crb); Peter Zijlstra (cla); cokemomo (cb). **Alamy Stock Photo:** Pulsar Images (tr). **76 123RF.com:** Alexander Romanov (tl). **Alamy Stock Photo:** Danny Smythe (cb). **Cover images: Front: 123RF.com:** Inacio Pires br; **Getty Images:** Ken Davies b.

All other images © Dorling Kindersley

For further information see: www.dkimages.com

Andre, aged 11, Australia

Meet children from around the world and find out about the foods that unite all of us.